Mysterious Encounters

Area 51

by Gail B. Stewart

KIDHAVEN PRESS
A part of Gale, Cengage Learning

Detroit • New York • San Francisco • New Haven, Conn • Waterville, Maine • London

GALE
CENGAGE Learning

LIBRARY OF CONGRESS CATALOGING-IN-PUBLICATION DATA

Stewart, Gail B. (Gail Barbara), 1949-
 Area 51 / by Gail B. Stewart.
    p. cm. — (Mysterious encounters)
 Includes bibliographical references and index.
 ISBN 978-0-7377-4410-1 (hardcover)
 1. Unidentified flying objects. 2. Area 51 (Nev.)—Juvenile literature. I. Title.
 TL789.2.S73 2009
 001.942—dc22
                                                                2008052921

KidHaven Press
27500 Drake Rd.
Farmington Hills, MI 48331

ISBN-13: 978-0-7377-4410-1
ISBN-10: 0-7377-4410-3

Printed by Bang Printing, Brainerd, MN, 3rd Ptg., 08/2010

Contents

Chapter 1

The Most
Secret Place
on Earth

The desert of south-central Nevada seems empty. There are very few towns. There are cactus plants, coyotes, rattlesnakes, and lots of sand. That is about all—or so it appears. But hidden between the mountains at the southern shore of a dry lake bed called Groom Lake, 90 miles (145km) north of the busy city of Las Vegas, is what some say is the most secretive place on the planet. It is a military base whose name is not known, although people have referred to it as Dreamland, the Ranch, and most often, Area 51.

Area 51 is a very small section of land lying within the U.S. Air Force's Nellis Range. Nellis

Area 51 is located within the United States Air Force's Nellis Range in the desert of south-central Nevada.

is a 4,687 square mile (12,139sq. km) area where pilots are trained for combat. Area 51 is so cloaked in mystery that for years the U.S. government did not even admit it exists. In fact, it does not appear on any map. Pilots are strictly forbidden to fly over it, even air force pilots flying out of Nellis. There are believed to be more than 1,000 people working there. The government requires that the workers sign an **oath** not to discuss any part of their jobs— even with their own families.

Cameras, Sensors, and "Cammo Dudes"

One of the most interesting clues about the secrecy of Area 51 is its security. There are no tall fences or barbed wire. But there are large signs posted on the **perimeter** of the area warning that it is a restricted area and anyone caught trespassing could be shot. Taking photographs or making sketches of the area is forbidden, too.

The warnings are backed up by other security measures around Area 51. There are lots of closed-

Security is very tight at Area 51. Large warning signs are posted around the area warning people that it is a restricted area and photography is prohibited.

circuit cameras that monitor the area. Some are easy to spot, and others are hidden in tall cactus plants. There are sensors under the desert sand that can detect motion and vibration. These sensors are said to be so accurate that they can distinguish between a human and one of the wild burros or coyotes that wander the Nevada desert.

If anyone tries to cross over into Area 51, he or she will be shocked at the response. Within seconds, armed guards instantly appear in white Jeeps. Because of the camouflage they wear, these guards are known to local residents as "Cammo Dudes."[1] They will **confiscate** sketches, cameras, and film— even from people standing outside the perimeter.

Too Much Secrecy?

Keeping something like Area 51 a secret can be tricky, especially in a democracy like the United States. The more the government tries to hide information, the more curious and suspicious people become. Is it all right for a government to keep secrets from its citizens? If so, what sorts of secrets are allowed? Those are questions about which people have different opinions.

"They'll Grab You"

People living nearby know very well how serious the Cammo Dudes are. Pat Travis is a resident of the tiny town of Rachel, just 12 miles (19km) away. She recalls a man who got in trouble for just reaching over the perimeter to grab a souvenir rock. When he did, sirens blared, searchlights went on, and security guards surrounded him. "Remember," says Travis, "if even as much as your toe gets inside the restricted area, they'll grab you."[2]

A woman walks near the entrance to the Area 51 research center in Rachel, Nevada. Many individuals have attempted to get near the perimeter and have been surrounded by security guards or buzzed by helicopters flying overhead.

Another resident, Chuck Clark, says that not only are the guards armed, but he believes they also have the ability to listen to conversations taking place in cars outside the perimeter. "Once I spoke to one of [the guards]," he says. "He repeated to me everything I had said in a car three miles down the road—the result of powerful directional microphones which are another tool in their arsenal."[3]

Many visitors to the area have even reported being buzzed by military helicopters. There is a rule in the military that helicopters cannot be flown less than 500 feet (152m) from the ground (except when taking off or landing). But when pilots think people are getting too close to the boundary of Area 51, they swoop down. The powerful **rotors** throw up showers of rocks and sand, sending visitors running for cover.

Mark Farmer has spent a long time gathering information about Area 51. He says that with such security, it is easy to understand why no one has yet been able to sneak into Area 51 for a closer look. "As far as we know," says Farmer, "nobody's ever been able to penetrate the base, and somebody would have to be extra stupid to try."[4]

UFOs at Area 51?

It is true that U.S. military bases need security. However, no base in the world has anything resembling the security at Area 51. That makes many people curious. They wonder what could be so

A Skeptical View

A skeptic is someone who doubts a particular story. Many people are skeptics when it comes to Area 51. They say the idea of UFOs at the base is ridiculous. The strange lights and sighting of unusual objects in the sky, they believe, are not flying saucers, but high-tech aircraft.

secret that such extreme measures as powerful microphones and warnings to shoot trespassers are necessary.

There are lots of theories. One is that the U.S. government has captured or retrieved UFOs and maybe even the aliens onboard. Some have suggested that American military technicians are studying the UFOs in order to copy the technology. In fact, a man who claimed to have worked at Area 51 has described in detail the experiments that have been conducted there.

Betty Lewis, a former Las Vegas resident, says:

I saw an interview on television with this man—Bob Lazar was his name. Everyone was talking about it, I mean *everybody*. He was an extremely believable young man—very smart, and not someone you'd believe was making things up for attention, you know? He said that the government was learning things about space travel, and how to apply that same technology to our own systems, I guess. But anyway, we were keeping those UFOs there, and even studying the bodies of the dead aliens.[5]

Classified

But others say the idea of UFOs at Area 51 is ridiculous. They think the explanation is far less bizarre than flying saucers. Instead, they believe, the U.S. government is developing and testing supersecret

Some individuals think that UFOs are being studied at Area 51, while others believe that the United States government is developing and testing weapons there.

weapons there. The secrecy, they say, is necessary for the security of the United States.

The U.S. government will not say one way or another. It denies that anything unusual or strange is occurring there but will not explain the secrecy. "Some specific activities and operations conducted on the Nellis Range remain **classified**," said an Air Force spokesman, "and cannot be discussed."[6]

The refusal of the government to even talk about Area 51 is confusing. No other military facility is so secretive. Is it actually possible that there is something (or someone) from outer space there? To find answers, it is helpful to take a look back and see how the mystery began.

Chapter 2

The Seeds of the Mystery

The facility known as Area 51 was created during the **cold war**. This was a time after World War II, when the Soviet Union (now Russia) and the United States were in conflict. Both countries prepared themselves for war by creating new weapons and spying on one another.

Skunk Works and the U-2

In the 1950s, the U.S. military suspected that the Soviet Union was producing many nuclear weapons. It wanted to know how many weapons the Soviets had. It also wanted to know where these weapons were being set up. The trouble was, the

In order to spy on the Soviet Union, the CIA approached Lockheed, an aircraft manufacturer, to build a plane that could fly higher than other planes. They developed the U-2, shown here in 1960, which could fly up to 75,000 feet.

U.S. military had no good way to find out. American military pilots could not fly over Soviet air space to investigate, because the Soviets would launch missiles to shoot the planes down.

The U.S. Central Intelligence Agency (CIA) approached a U.S. aircraft manufacturer called Lockheed to build a special plane. The CIA needed a plane that could fly higher than other planes. That way they could spy on the Soviets without being attacked. But secrecy was very important. If the Soviets learned about the new plane, they might develop their own planes that could also fly very high.

Lockheed had a special secret department called Skunk Works. Its technicians developed the U-2.

It was a plane that could fly higher than any other plane—up to 75,000 feet (22,860m). The CIA hoped the U-2 could fly over the Soviet Union, take pictures with high-powered cameras, and return home without being attacked. First, however, it was important to find a place to test the new plane.

A "Lead Overcoat"

The CIA knew it could not test the U-2 at existing Air Force bases. Soviet spies might be watching. So the CIA looked around for a location for a secret test site. It found one at Groom Lake, a round, dry lake bed that had been used to test nuclear weapons. Old government maps show the nuclear testing ground divided into numbered areas, and this particular spot was number 51.

The CIA tested the U-2 at Groom Lake, a round, dry lake bed that had been used to test nuclear weapons. Pictured here is a satellite view of Groom Lake.

It was big enough and very remote. And because the area contained so much **fallout** from the nuclear testing, no one would be foolish enough to wander around the area. Extensive background checks were conducted on the handful of men hired as test pilots for the U-2. They had to take lie detector tests, too. They did not even use their real names, but instead used **aliases**.

Workers hired to build a makeshift air base for the planes and the pilots hired to fly the actual missions were kept in the dark, too. The crews were not told what they were building or how the area was to be used. The CIA did not want anyone talking about what he or she was doing in the Nevada

Francis Gary Powers

Pilot Francis Gary Powers was captured when his U-2 plane was shot down over the Soviet Union. He was put on trial there for spying and was sent to a Soviet prison. Two years later he was part of a swap, exchanged for a Soviet spy in a U.S. prison. While he was in prison, Powers kept a secret journal of his experiences. The journal is now on display at the Smithsonian Institution Museum in Washington, D.C.

desert. One worker later told researcher Phil Patton that not being able to tell his family what he was working on felt like a "lead overcoat . . . a constant weight."[7]

Shot Down

To keep the site secret, President Dwight D. Eisenhower signed an executive order in 1955, restricting the air space over Groom Lake. No planes—military, commercial, or private—were allowed to fly over it. Three years later, in 1958, he signed another order, making the 60 square miles (115sq. km) around Groom Lake officially nonexistent. Someone looking at a map of the area would find the names of no mountains, roads, or other landmarks.

But the Soviet Union had spies throughout the world. They learned about the U-2 and developed a special missile that could be released high enough to shoot down one of the new planes. It happened on May 1, 1960, just days before an important international **summit** between the two countries. The Soviet Union realized the U-2 was a spy plane and was angry with the United States. As a result, it canceled the summit.

The United States did not want to admit it had been spying. President Eisenhower assured the American people that the United States had not been spying. The plane shot down by the Soviets, said Eisenhower, was only a weather research plane.

But the Soviets had retrieved the U-2 and captured its pilot. They found the powerful camera with which he had taken pictures of their missile sites. As a result, the U.S. government was embarrassed, for it had been caught in a lie. The incident created a dangerous rift between the two countries. In addition, the American people were angry that their government had lied to them.

More Secrets

Instead of ending its program of spying on the Soviets, the CIA increased it. Over the next few years, several new planes were tested and fine-tuned at Area 51. One was a more powerful spy plane that could fly higher and faster than the U-2. Known as the A-12 Blackbird, the sleek black plane could fly 90,000 feet (27,432m) above the earth. It could fly three times faster than the speed of sound, so if it was detected, it could easily escape any warplanes that tried to shoot it down.

After the A-12 came a series of new planes, each that could fly faster and higher than the last. With each new project, new hangars and larger fuel tanks were needed. All those improvements meant more workers at Area 51. As always, secrecy was intense. People working on one project were not allowed to see what was going on with other projects. In fact, when a particular crew brought their test plane out of a hangar, the other crews were ordered to go inside, so that they could not see it.

Visitors walk beneath a Lockheed A-12 Blackbird jet at the Intrepid Sea-Air-Space Museum in New York. The A-12 Blackbird was a spy plane that could fly as high as 90,000 feet and could fly three times faster than the speed of sound.

But Area 51 had another use besides testing new top-secret planes. It was also the place where the military would bring enemy planes that it or its **al-lies** had shot down or captured. For example, several Soviet jets, called MiGs, were secretly trucked into the Nevada desert after being shot down and retrieved in the Middle East by Israel. At Area 51, experts took them apart and studied the technol-

ogy. "Learning what our enemies were doing was really important," says pilot Jeff de Silva. "Anytime you can see firsthand how the Soviets were designing their warplanes, that becomes extremely valuable for improving our own designs."[8]

Black Projects

The work being done at Area 51 became more and more secretive over the years. New designs of top-secret aircraft are known as "black projects." As the name suggests, these are highly classified. Even most high-ranking government and military officials are not told about these projects. The money for such projects is not reviewed by Congress, but rather comes

High Flying

One of the dangers of flying in the U-2 planes was the altitude, or height at which the planes flew. That far above the ground, there is very little oxygen. The first U-2 pilots at Area 51 almost certainly had to learn how to use an oxygen mask while flying at high altitudes, so they did not black out and crash.

The work being done at Area 51 is extremely secretive and highly classified.

out of a secret pool of money called a black budget. "The existence of the [black project] program and its purpose is secret," writes aviation expert Bill Sweetman. "That's what makes them black—they don't officially exist."[9]

Bits and pieces have leaked out. There are stories of altitude and speed records being set, and test pilots achieving things that no one ever believed possible. There are believed to be supersecret, strange-looking planes that can go anywhere in the world in less than two hours. But the most bizarre stories are not about jet fighters or test pilots. Instead, these stories have to do with aliens and UFOs—and these stories come from a man who saw them at Area 51.

Chapter 3

UFOs at Area 51?

F or years, people who visited or lived near Area 51 knew there was something very unusual going on there. They would see strange lights in the sky at night—and the object did not behave as a plane would. "One of [the objects] was cigar-shaped, with big orange glowing lights and a bright white ball underneath. It was as big as a 747 [airplane], and I saw it from a quarter mile away," says Las Vegas resident Kathleen Ford. "I stepped back saying to myself, 'Oh my God, oh my God,' and then it hung for a second before becoming invisible."[10]

The strange lights in the night sky over Area 51 created a great deal of conversation. But there was no one to ask about what people were seeing. At least, that was the case before May 1989. That is when a Las Vegas television reporter named George Knapp did an interview with Bob Lazar, a scientist who said he had worked at Area 51. He told Knapp that work on new fighter jets was just part of what was happening at Area 51.

Aliens and Saucers

Bob Lazar said he was offered a job at the secret base in 1988 because of his work as a scientist. He told reporter George Knapp how he had been required to sign a very strict security agreement before beginning his job. He agreed to allow the government to tap his phone. He also agreed that his home and his car could be searched without warning at any time. Finally, he promised that he

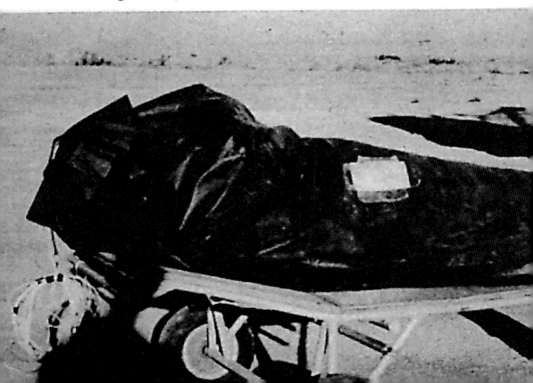

would not talk to anyone about what he saw at the base.

Lazar said that he was taken to a special section of the base called S-4 by a bus with blacked-out windows. Then a military officer gave him a stack of blue folders and told Lazar to read them carefully. Lazar says that what he read astonished him.

He saw photographs of nine discs, which he first assumed must be new military weapons of some kind. However, he turned a page and saw other photographs—these of strange-looking creatures on whom the government had performed **autopsies**. The creatures had grayish skin, large heads, and big, dark eyes. Lazar realized with a shock that the discs were not military weapons. The U.S. military had in its possession actual flying saucers, as well as a few of the aliens who piloted them.

Bob Lazer, a scientist who said he had worked at Area 51, told reporters that he saw photographs of strange-looking creatures on whom the government had performed autopsies. This photo comes from "The Roswell Report," which discusses how test dummies were put in insulation bags. Witnesses thought that these were alien victims.

ET Highway

Rumors about UFOs above Area 51 resulted in lots of tourists pouring into Nevada. To add to the public interest, Nevada governor Bob Smith even renamed Highway 375 the "Extraterrestrial Highway." Smith had official-looking road signs warning "Speed Limit Warp 7" and "Alien Crossing" posted along the route.

Taking the Saucers Apart

Lazar was told that his job was called "reverse engineering." That means he had to take one of the saucers apart to learn how it worked. Then the military could use that same technology to build their own new planes. Excited at the idea of being part of this secret project, Lazar got right to work.

Only about half of the nine discs at S-4 worked at all, and the rest had been damaged somehow. In his interview with Knapp, Lazar recalled how excited he was to watch one of the working discs for the first time:

It was just about dusk. I came out of the door that was outside the hangar, which led to a hallway . . . and the disc was already outside.

Whether they carried it out or flew it out, I don't know. I was sitting on the ground. Right off to the side there was a guy with a scanner. The first thing, I was told to stand by him and not go anywhere else. . . .

The disc sat out there for a period of time, then the bottom of it glowed blue and it began to hiss. . . . It lifted off the ground, quietly, except for that little hiss in the background, and that stopped as soon as it reached about twenty or thirty feet. It shifted off to the left, shifted over to the right, and set back down. I mean, it doesn't sound like much, but it was incredibly impressive, just—mind boggling.[11]

Too Much Security

Lazar says that he discovered fairly soon that the project would only have limited success. One problem was that the power source of the discs was a strange dark-orange material that he had never seen before. He named it Element 115, because it contained 115 **protons**. But Element 115 did not exist on Earth. Without that special power source, it would be hard to use the alien technology for U.S. planes.

Even more important, Lazar says, is that secrecy got in the way of good research. He believes that there was too much emphasis on security and not enough on sharing ideas with other scientists at

Highway 375, also called the "Extraterrestrial Highway," is the closest road to Area 51. Lazar and a friend drove up Highway 375 to see if tests on a disc that were supposed to take place actually did.

S-4. For example, Lazar says, he was not allowed to talk with any other workers except his supervisor. He was never allowed to walk around the area by himself. He says he was even accompanied by security guards when he went to the bathroom.

Although he had signed a security agreement not to tell anyone what he was working on, Lazar confided in his best friend one day. His friend was somewhat doubtful, so one night Lazar and his friend drove up Highway 375, the closest road to Area 51. Lazar knew that a disc was going to be tested that night. Sure enough, reports researcher David Darlington, as the two friends sat along the desert highway, they watched as a brightly lit craft darted around the mountains before disappearing.

Is His Story True?

Eventually, Bob Lazar was fired. His supervisor learned that he had broken his security agreement. Lazar was afraid of what might happen to him, however, so he decided to go public with his story. However, after his television interview with George Knapp aired, many people were skeptical of his claims.

Doubting Lazar

Some of the things Bob Lazar claimed made many people doubt his truthfulness. For instance, he said he had graduated from two colleges, but when reporters checked Lazar's story, those schools had never heard of him. His explanation was that the government had erased his identity to make him look like a liar. Some people believed that, but others were even more doubtful.

For one thing, Lazar claimed to have graduated from two different colleges, but neither school had any record of his attendance. On the other hand, he was clearly a man who had a scientific background. One only needed to talk with him for a few minutes to realize he knew a great deal about **physics**. Some critics say that it is unlikely that Lazar would have been hired to do such top-secret work. Why would an unknown civilian be trusted by the S-4 military leaders to work on such a highly classified project?

But the most common reason for doubt was simply the nature of Lazar's story. Many people did not believe that the U.S. government actually had UFOs and aliens at a military base. Lazar himself admits the story seems unbelievable. "Given the same information, I'm not sure I would believe the story either," he says. "There's a lot I can't prove. It's what I observed and what happened to me."[12]

An Excited Public

After Lazar's interview, people began to flock to the area around Groom Lake. At night they gathered at the place along the highway where Lazar said that the discs could sometimes be seen. During the day, they hiked up the mountain known as Freedom Ridge, 12 miles (19km) east of Groom Lake, just in case they could get a glimpse of something happening. Large buses brought tourists from Las Vegas. They came to Rachel, the tiny town nearest Area 51, to buy souvenir mugs and T-shirts decorated

Tourists began flocking to Groom Lake after Lazar's interview. Souvenir shops in Rachel, Nevada capitalized on this by selling mugs and T-shirts decorated with pictures of aliens and UFOs.

with pictures of aliens and UFOs.

But the military was not amused. It was unhappy with the attention being paid to Area 51. It refused to answer any questions about what was going on out in the Nevada desert. And it quickly got permission to seize another 4,000 acres (1,619ha) of land around the base, including Freedom Ridge, to keep any more tourists from seeing what was going on. Whatever was happening at Area 51 was going to remain secret.

Chapter 4

Trouble at Area 51

For decades, the U.S. government never admitted that Area 51 was a real place, refusing to verify that the base actually existed. It was finally forced to admit the truth—or at least part of it—because of the strange, unexplained deaths of workers at the base.

"My Face Is on Fire"

It was in 1989 that the first problems arose at Area 51. A sheet-metal worker named Robert Frost became very ill. His skin began getting scaly and peeling off. His wife later recalled how he came home from work one day in pain. "He was scream-

Workers at Area 51 started getting sick, which they believed resulted from dealing with hazardous waste at Area 51.

ing, 'My face is on fire,'" she recalls. "His face was bright red and swollen up like a basketball."[13]

Nothing seemed to relieve his pain, and soon the problems spread across his body. He died a year later, and doctors performed an **autopsy**. They found high levels of poisons throughout his body. They believed that Frost had been exposed to very dangerous chemicals at work.

By the mid-1990s, more workers had become sick with the same painful symptoms. They believed they got ill from dealing with hazardous waste at Area 51. Doctors were unable to cure them. Without knowing what sorts of chemicals the workers had been exposed to, the doctors did not know how to treat them. The workers asked their supervisors at Area 51 to tell their doctors about the chemicals they had been exposed to, but the workers were told that the information was classified. The contents of the waste were top secret. Frustrated, the sick workers finally contacted a lawyer, Jonathan Turley. They hoped Turley could help them get the information the doctors needed. And what the men told Turley astonished him.

"These Are Very Patriotic People"

The men explained to Turley that on occasion they had been ordered to dispose of waste from the base. They were told to dig huge trenches. Then

The Little A'Le'Inn

One place that has benefited from the UFO rumors at Area 51 is a tiny bar and grill nearby. After Bob Lazar told his story and tourists began coming to the region, the owners changed their bar and grill's name to the Little A'Le'Inn (as in Little Alien). In addition to food, it sells alien mugs and T-shirts and is a gathering place for people who are interested in sharing their stories about what is happening at Area 51.

they dumped large numbers of 55-gallon drums containing chemical waste from Area 51 into the trenches. When each trench was full, they would douse the drums with jet fuel and then use a flare to set them ablaze.

Turley was amazed at the government's decision to break **environmental** laws that prohibited the burning of toxic material. "There's a reason why burning hazardous waste is a crime," he said later. "And the reason is that most hazardous waste is more dangerous when you burn it, because it's an easier way to enter the human body."[14]

It appeared that the gases created from the burning hazardous waste had poisoned the men, killing Frost and one other worker. The sick workers, as well as the widows of the two men who had died, filed a lawsuit against the government. They were not seeking money, Turley explained, but information about the hazardous waste so their doctors could make them well. "These are not the type of people who look to lawyers and courts to resolve their problems," he said. "These are very patriotic people. They were put at Area 51 for a reason. And things had to get very, very bad for them to seek help."[15]

The Base That Does Not Exist

The lawsuit did not go well. When the trial began in 1994, the government claimed that there was no Area 51. It said that it did not appear on any maps.

Therefore, if the base did not officially exist, then the workers themselves did not exist. And so the government did not have to supply any information about material that was or was not burned there.

But Turley showed the judge pay stubs of the workers. The stubs identified the facility as Area 51. He also had found references to Area 51 in Defense Department memos. Refusing to admit that the place even existed, he said, was ridiculous. Eventually, the government had to admit Area 51 was a real place. But it said that to give out any more information would threaten national security. Some of the waste that was discarded and burned might have consisted of special chemicals used to make top-secret planes or weapons. By giving out the names of those ingredients, the government would also be providing the information to America's enemies. In 1996, the judge ruled that there was not

In response to a lawsuit, the government finally admitted that Area 51 did exist, but it wouldn't give out any more information because it said that it would threaten national security.

John Does

When the sick workers decided to sue the U.S. government, they were nervous. They had signed an oath of secrecy when they accepted their jobs, so they worried that they might lose their retirement pensions (money paid to workers after they retire) by suing. So Jonathan Turley helped them file their lawsuit using the name John Doe for each of them, so they did not have to use their real names.

enough evidence to prove that the government was responsible for the workers' illness. Turley appealed the ruling, taking his case to the U.S. Supreme Court in 1998, but was unsuccessful.

The Mystery Goes On

The trial proved that there was an Area 51. But people were unable to learn anything about what really went on there. In the years since that trial, many still speculate about what could be so secret about Area 51 that the government would be willing to risk workers' lives.

Experts say there are many rumors about the kinds of aircraft being developed there. One common rumor is that Skunk Works developed a plane called the Aurora. According to aviation expert Bill Sweetman, the $15 billion Aurora can travel at least five times the speed of sound and can reach anywhere on Earth in only a few hours. The white trail it leaves in the sky, called a **contrail**, has the look of a "doughnut on a rope,"[16] say some who have caught glimpses of the plane over the Nevada desert. Whatever is being tested at Area 51 is very fast, as proven by the increasing number of **sonic booms**. According to newspaper reporter Bill Hendrick, sonic booms over Area 51 are "as common as sirens in a big city."[17]

There are many rumors about the kinds of aircraft being developed at Area 51. One rumor is that there is a plane called the Aurora that can reach anywhere on Earth in only a few hours, can travel at five times the speed of sound, and leaves contrails in the sky resembling a "doughnut on a rope."

But while few doubt that a lot of activity is due to the testing of secret aircraft, many are still convinced that the UFO connection to Area 51 is undeniable. "What you see here isn't all good old American technology," insists one long-time resident of Rachel. "I saw something last night, a bunch of orange and red lights in a horizontal row. The thing just hung there and zipped off, straight up. I don't care what people think. If you see it, you'll believe."[18]

While the government refuses to offer any answers, one thing is certain—there is *something* happening at Area 51. Whether it has to do with alien technology or black-budget military projects, those secrets continue to puzzle and intrigue lots of people.

Notes

Chapter 1: The Most Secret Place on Earth

1. David Darlington, *Area 51 The Dreamland Chronicles: The Legend of America's Most Secret Military Base*. New York: Holt, 1997, p. 24.
2. Quoted in Maxim Kniazkov, "Aliens Welcome: Town Serves as Landing Strip for UFO Theorists," *Washington Times*, January 17, 2007.
3. Quoted in Alan Hall, "Alien Highway," *Daily Mirror* (London), July 10, 1996.
4. Quoted in History Channel, "Area 51: Beyond Top Secret," DVD, A&E Home Video, 2005.
5. Telephone interview, Betty Lewis, October 12, 2008.
6. Quoted in Elisabeth Deffner, "UFO Mystery," *National Geographic for Kids*, March 2008, p. 24.

Chapter 2: The Seeds of the Mystery

7. Quoted in "Area 51: Beyond Top Secret."
8. Personal interview, Jeff de Silva, Bloomington, MN, October 18, 2008.
9. Quoted in "Area 51: Beyond Top Secret."

Chapter 3: UFOs at Area 51?

10. Quoted in Hall, "Alien Highway."
11. Quoted in Darlington, *Area 51 The Dreamland Chronicles*, p. 73.
12. Quoted in George Knapp, "Bob Lazar: The Man Behind Area 51," *Las Vegas Now Eyewitness News*, May 23, 2005, www.klas-tv.com/Global/story.asp?S=3369879.

Chapter 4: Trouble at Area 51

13. Quoted in Malcolm Howard, "Environment of Secrecy," *Amicus Journal*, Spring 1997, p. 34.
14. Quoted in "Area 51: Beyond Top Secret."
15. Quoted in "Area 51: Beyond Top Secret."
16. Phil Patton, *Dreamland: Travels Inside the Secret World of Roswell and Area 51*, New York: Villard, 1998, p. 42.
17. Bill Hendrick, "The Mysteries of Aliens and Area 51," *Atlanta Journal-Constitution*, June 29, 1997.
18. Quoted in Hendrick, "The Mysteries of Aliens and Area 51."

Glossary

aliases: False names.

allies: Nations that have agreed to remain loyal to one another.

autopsy: A medical examination of a body after death.

classified: Highly secret.

cold war: The time after World War II when there was a great deal of tension between the United States and the Soviet Union. Because they were not engaged in actual combat with military forces, the war was called "cold."

confiscate: To seize.

contrail: The white trail in the sky that a jet creates as it flies.

environmental: Having to do with keeping land, water, and air clean.

fallout: The very dangerous particles left after a nuclear explosion.

oath: A solemn promise.

perimeter: The outward boundary of an area.

physics: The science of matter, energy, and motion.

protons: The positive particles that are part of an atom.

rotors: The large blades of a helicopter.

sonic booms: The loud noises heard on the ground when airplanes fly faster than the speed of sound.

summit: A high-level meeting between the leaders of nations.

For Further Exploration

Books

Jack David, *U-2 Planes*. Minneapolis, MN: Bell-wether Media, 2008. This is a short but very interesting book describing the various types of American military planes used in spying missions. It contains a very helpful index, as well as a bibliography.

Peggy J. Parks, *Aliens*. Farmington Hills, MI: Kid-Haven Press, 2007. A very readable introduction to the idea of visitors from outer space on Earth. It includes a helpful glossary and Web sites for further exploration.

Curt Sutherly, *UFO Mysteries: A Reporter Seeks the Truth*. St. Paul, MN: Llewellyn, 2001. Although written for an adult audience, good readers can enjoy chapter 8, in which the author tells of visiting the perimeter of Area 51.

Internet Source

George Knapp, "Bob Lazar: The Man Behind Area 51," *Las Vegas Now Eyewitness News*, May 23, 2005, www.klas-tv.com/Global/story.asp?S=3369879.

Web Sites

Area51ZONE.com (www.area51zone.com). This Web site focuses on the various planes that have been tested at Area 51 over the years. It includes photographs of some of what may be the Aurora and other "black projects" that are rumored to fly out of Area 51.

Dreamland Resort (www.dreamlandresort.com). This site has excellent photographs taken from recent satellite flyovers. It also has links to a variety of newspaper and magazine articles about the base.

SchoolHistory.co.uk (www.schoolhistory.co.uk/lessons/coldwar/coldwar_u2.html). This is an interactive site which includes a page titled "U-2 incident—1960," where students can learn about the U-2 incident and later quiz themselves on how well they understand it and its effect on the cold war.

UFO Evidence (www.ufoevidence.org). This is the largest site on the Internet for information, discussions, and photographic evidence of current UFO sightings and reports. There also fascinating information on how researchers investigate UFO sightings.

UFOWhipnet.org (http://ufo.whipnet.org). This site offers information about the history and current use of Area 51, including a huge number of links.

Index

Picture Credits

About the Author

Gail B. Stewart is the author of more than 200 books for children and young adults. The parent of three sons, she and her husband live in Minneapolis, Minnesota.